720.973　　　ART　　X rec　87197
Johnson, P.
Philip Johnson.

PHILIP JOHNSON

Library of Contemporary Architects

PHILIP JOHNSON

Introduction and notes by
CHARLES NOBLE

with 62 photographs by
YUKIO FUTAGAWA

SIMON AND SCHUSTER NEW YORK

Copyright © 1972 by Thames and Hudson Ltd, London
Photographs copyright © 1968 by Yukio Futagawa

Published in the United States by Simon and Schuster
Rockefeller Center, 630 Fifth Avenue
New York, New York 10020

First published in Japan in 1968 by Bijutsu Shuppan-sha, Tokyo, in their series
GENDAI KENCHIKUKA SHIRIZU.
New texts have been provided for this English language edition.

First U.S. printing

SBN 671-21249-4
Library of Congress Catalog Card Number: 74-185065

Printed in Japan

Contents

Introduction

Although in the public mind the idea of struggle is indissolubly wedded to that of achievement, particularly in creative matters, it is a disturbing fact that not all the great artists of history languished in obscurity until their works attained posthumous fame. For every Cézanne whose canvases once changed hands for *sous*, there is a Picasso who attained fame and fortune well before middle age; for every Ho Chi Minh who achieved immense power and adulation after washing dishes in London during his youth, there is the able son of a wealthy man who gains political power almost as a matter of course. The history of the modern movement in architecture abounds with such paradoxes: middle-aged, *émigré* Germans cast out of their own country by the Nazis later attained world fame in the United States, while the native son of a lawyer who became an architect only in his late thirties (after a successful career as a critic) attained comparable fame inside ten years. Philip Johnson, whose career might be encapsulated thus, is the lawyer's son—Mies van der Rohe the *émigré* German. In the case of these two men the paradox is instructive because they were friends as well as pupil and master.

Johnson was born in 1906 in Cleveland, Ohio, when Mies van der Rohe was already twenty and working in Berlin for the leading German furniture designer Bruno Paul. During the young Johnson's childhood and youth Mies worked for Peter Behrens (as at one time or another did Walter Gropius and Le Corbusier) and served four years as a private soldier in the German army. By the time Johnson had graduated from Harvard after reading classics, the largely self-taught Mies was Vice-President of the *Deutscher Werkbund* and was immersed in the organization of the famous Weissenhof exhibition of modern housing held at Stuttgart in 1927. One year later the two met for the first time, Johnson on a visit to Europe as a young graduate, Mies—by Johnson's own account—'starving to death in an attic in Berlin'.[1] This description is almost certainly an exaggeration and probably reflects Johnson's transatlantic affluence rather than Mies' poverty, which was in any case relative at a time when the number of unemployed in Germany had already climbed above four million. Mies was single and at the time was still working on his legendary masterpiece, the German pavilion for the Barcelona exhibition of 1929. On his return to the United States Johnson was a confirmed enthusiast for the new architecture he had seen and, in collaboration with the critic Henry-Russell Hitchcock, he prepared a book on the subject called *The International Style: Architecture since 1922*. The name stuck,[2] as did the career Johnson had chosen at the

Department of Architecture at the Rockefeller-financed Museum of Modern Art, New York. Throughout the Depression years in America Johnson maintained and widened his connection with modern architects in Europe, and organized exhibitions on contemporary themes at the museum, including one in 1933 entitled 'The Birth of the American Skyscraper'. In this as in other cases a resolutely stylistic view was taken of a ruthlessly economic and technical subject. Le Corbusier's first visit to the United States in 1935/36 was arranged by Hitchcock and Johnson and, although it ended in acrimonious disputes about money, it presaged the arrival of yet more Europeans. Among these was Walter Gropius, former Principal of the Bauhaus, who in 1937 became Chairman of the Harvard Design School. In the same year Johnson himself engineered the first visit of Mies van der Rohe in order to negotiate a commission for the design of a house for Mr and Mrs Stanley Resor in Wyoming. The commission fell through but chance encounters in Chicago led to Mies being offered the Directorship of the Armour Institute School of Architecture, later to become the architectural faculty of the Illinois Institute of Technology. At the age of 52 Mies accepted and, returning to Germany to wind up his affairs there, he left his native country forever in 1938; he had been unable to obtain commissions in Europe since the closure of the Bauhaus in 1933 and had subsisted more or less on royalties from the continuing production of patented tubular steel chairs which he had designed ten years before.

In 1941 Philip Johnson returned to Harvard as a student under Gropius and Marcel Breuer, another ex-Bauhaus personality already well known in the United States for the design of small houses. Gropius espoused concepts of creative teamwork which were utterly foreign to Johnson's already highly developed design sense and although no direct conflict between them occurred—Gropius' retiring nature and Johnson's urbanity conspired to make such an event unlikely—the eminent pupil, already well known as a critic and historian, learned more from Breuer than for his prestigious Chairman. Johnson's first practical architectural work dates from this period at Harvard; the house he built for himself at Cambridge, Mass., in 1942 clearly shows the influence of Breuer, but more clearly still hints at the type of house Mies had originally planned for the American clients Johnson had found for him in the late 1930s (a type which Mies himself was unable to build until the ten-year gestation period of the glass box ended with the completion of the Farnsworth house in 1951).[3] As in later dwellings, Johnson chose for his first architectural realization furniture by Mies van der Rohe— none of it designed after 1930.

Following his graduation at the age of 37 Johnson immediately volunteered for the army; his period of service was short and, apparently, undistinguished. His two biographers[4] do not allude to it, and he himself only once referred to it, in an interview given in 1970, as having shown him that the treatment of Negroes in the United States had indeed become better and not worse during the intervening years.[5]

In 1946 Johnson returned to the Museum of Modern Art, New York, as Director of the Department of Architecture and Design and in the same year completed his first private commission, a house for Eugene Farney at Sagaponack, Long Island, New York. Here, although the timber cladding and raised profile unquestionably evoked the domestic feeling of Breuer's work in the same genre, the planning and furnishing of the building as before obediently echoed the restraint and asceticism of Mies. In future years Johnson was to make much of the sheer multiplicity of such tell-tale origins and influences, for him the correct response to charges of plagiarism was always to multiply the alleged offence and expose it as in reality a form of homage. In time these influences became more and more widely spaced over the whole spectrum of modern architecture, with the result that charges of historicism and eclecticism[6] succeeded earlier slighting references to derivation. As this latter circumstance unfolded Johnson yet again revealed himself as more sophisticated and intelligent than his critics. The advantages of having an established reputation before an established practice were to become clearer year by year.

At the time of the Farney house, however, Johnson was still what his former mentor and collaborator Henry-Russell Hitchcock called a 'timid' designer. His correctness knew no bounds. Having been instrumental in the popularization of the International Style in the United States, and having contrived both to *adopt as his protégé* and *be the protégé of* its undisputed master, Mies van der Rohe, Johnson proceeded to reinforce the foundations of Mies' career by writing a book on his architecture. The work,[7] published by the Museum of Modern Art in 1947, eventually ran to two editions and was influential in establishing Mies' commercial career in the United States. With the standing derived from his official position at the Museum of Modern Art and with an authentic modern pioneer behind him, Johnson devoted the decade after 1946 to learning the art and practice of architecture from Mies. He learned well and by the time Mies invited him to collaborate over the project for the Seagram Building in New York was already an established, practising architect as well as a critic and historian known for his dissenting voice on the subject of the meaning of architecture itself.

Johnson early developed an expertise in dealing with criticism, in fact through his success as critic and writer he developed it before substantive architectural works of his own were there to be criticized. The remarkable success of this posture was never more clearly evidenced than over the matter of the famous Glass House at New Canaan, Conn., which was completed in 1949.

The concept of a glass box, set *in* nature with natural vegetation and vistas as its real walls and boundaries, has its origins in the *Glasarchitektur* fantasies of the German pioneers of the early 1920s; patiently formalized by Mies during the years immediately preceding his emigration, it came to America with him in embryo form as an initial design study for the unrealized Resor house. In 1946, having found a client for such a dwelling in the person of Dr Farnsworth, Mies redesigned the box originally intended for mountainous country in Wyoming for a less wild site on the banks of the Fox River at Plano, Illinois. For various reasons connected with disputes and difficulties over cost the house was not completed until 1951, by which time Philip Johnson had his own glass box—built for himself—and it had been up for two years. There are of course differences between the two dwellings; Johnson's black steel structural frame recedes while the immediate surroundings of the house are carefully lawned with a view to outdoor living for part of the year. The Farnsworth house of the other hand features projecting, white-enamelled structural steel and is set, like a 'beached yacht'[8] on uncut *pelouse* with only a small rectangular travertine terrace alongside to serve as defined open space. Nonetheless the intended response to varying conditions of light and darkness was identical in both cases, the glass cubes alternately dissolve and reflect leaving either the landscape apparently barely disturbed, or the form of the house 'camouflaged' as by some kind of optical painting. This fundamental principle is undoubtedly a direct inheritance from Mies, while the formal similarity itself proceeds secondarily from a simple efficiency in terms of minimal structure and transparent geometry. In a review of the house published in a British architectural journal in 1950,[9] Johnson traced the derivation of the building through Schinkel, Choisy, Mies and others extending back as far as Palladian times. This long list was in part a characteristic refutation of the charge of plagiarism mentioned above. The house embodies more than Mies' optical idea; it also represents the beginnings of the exposition of a theory of 'processional' architecture which Johnson was to develop rapidly as his practice expanded into the area of public buildings. Visitors to the New Canaan house have frequently noted the indirect approach to, and delayed view of the house, which a rise in the ground ensures. Beyond this they have noted Johnson's habit of welcoming them from *in front* of the house rather than from the door; this he achieves by noting the arrival of a car some time before it can be seen. In both these factors—the delayed sight of the house itself and the presence of the welcoming figure in front of it—is to be found a clue to the meaning of Johnson's use of historical models as well as his perception of the role of architecture in relation to human life. Because Johnson sees a processional and ennobling basis to the process of *using* buildings, his architecture can borrow from the formal repertory of previous architectural epochs in a manner quite different from, say, the vulgar application of a pediment of 'Georgian' appearance to a suburban house. In the scale and grandeur of his architecture, particularly in its later and more grandiloquent manifestations, Johnson had echoed not merely the form of earlier styles, but the processional significance that was once an integral part of their use. When Philip Johnson welcomes visitors to his own summer palace at New Canaan, he does so in the full knowledge that their physical approach to it is as circumscribed as was that of an ambassador arriving at the Court of Imperial Rome. His grasp of status and movement within and without buildings is impeccable; even the solid guest house which counterpoints the transparent residence at New Canaan is not solid merely for this inconsequentially aesthetic reason, the see-through house confers an exhibitionistic status upon its occupant just as a girl in a see-through dress becomes the cynosure of all eyes. The guests are not to be ogled in this way, they are there to ogle. There is no short cut to Philip Johnson's presence—in the New Canaan house he even carries his garbage out through the front door.[10]

The astonishing impregnability of Johnson's position within five or six years of qualifying as an architect did not stop his regal use of space and distance: a teacher before he was a student, a talent scout before he ever displayed talent, a client before he was an architect, Johnson presented his critics and detractors, then as now, with a host of flexible and worldly strategies. Not for him the spectacle of successive owners bricking up windows, adding pitched roofs, or painting out designed colour, that had marked the passage of forty years in the case of Le Corbusier's famous houses at Pessac.[11] Not for him the encroachment of the highway authorities which has already brought feeder roads to within fifty yards of Mies' Farnsworth house. New Canaan will eternally rest under Johnson's control—indeed plans may already have been finalized to turn the house into a Philip Johnson Memorial Museum on his death. Johnson's mentor, who lived for thirty years in the same rented apartment in Chicago, took no such precautions; the Barcelona Pavilion stood for less than a year and after being dismantled its components were lost.

> 'Art has nothing to do with intellectual pursuit—it shouldn't be in a university at all. Art should be practised in gutters—pardon me, in attics.'[12]

Johnson's career as a critic and historian had led him early to the practice of public speaking, this side of his career faltered slightly during his second studentship but developed again as he gained confidence in his new career in the 1950s—as printed extracts reveal, he never attempted to emulate his master's cryptic style of speech. In 1950 he designed the annexe to the Museum of Modern Art in New York and between then and his invitation to join Mies in the design of the 39-storey Seagram Building in 1956 he completed a large number of small houses, all of them featuring combinations of solid and transparent rectangular geometry. 'All history disproves the idea that architecture is anything but an art', he wrote boldly in 1954; in the following year he embarked on a characteristic lampoon of Ruskin in his well-known 'Seven Crutches of Modern Architecture', a talk delivered to students at Harvard. Lurking behind the humour which pervades this address are some profound ideas on the nature of architectural practice which could only have come from a sensitive and intelligent man who came late to such labours with a broader knowledge derived from another career. Johnson early understood the infinitely devious process of evasion which the architect, in common with most truly creative workers, will employ in order to avoid the torment of actually doing the work he is supposed to do. An expert in evasions, he developed an eagle eye in detecting them—and a perverse pride in doing things the hard way himself. This pride carries through into his private as well as his professional life. In later years he became well known for not suffering fools gladly—and, it would appear, not even suffering his guests to place their own orders when dining with him in restaurants.[13]

According to Johnson the first of the 'seven crutches' by which architects evade their real responsibilities always used to be HISTORY, 'What do you mean you don't like my tower? There it is in Wren!' But, he conceded, it was no longer the crutch it had been. The second was the crutch of PRETTY DRAWING. 'Fundamentally architecture is something you build and put together, and people walk in and they like it. But that's too hard. Pretty pictures are easier.' (So too are articles on ecology, as he claimed in a later interview.[14]) The third crutch was more serious, it was UTILITY, and in his denunciation of it Johnson began his abandonment of the moral basis of the International Style.

> 'If the business of getting the house to run well takes precedence over your artistic invention the result won't be architecture at all; merely an assemblage of useful parts.'

There is an implied indictment of Le Corbusier's famous definition of a house in this extract. Whether a 'machine for living in' is architecture or 'merely an assemblage of useful parts' is a question never (apparently) directly asked. In his later years Johnson learned to avoid such mine-fields with a joke, 'Maybe we're in an anti-hero period which will last a thousand years. *Vive la différence*—let's go on and have fun',[15] but there is truth in the assertion that he always referred to Le Corbusier as the greatest 'designer' of all. Moral outrage on Johnson's part is conspicuously rare, as is any direct locking of horns with the stern, unbending ascetic spirit which unquestionably possessed many of the founders of modern architecture. The entire structure of the seven crutches bespeaks a thoroughly amoral and hedonistic grasping of the opportunities of eclecticism, together with a steadfast refusal to indulge in histrionic recitations of the cruelty of the muse. When asked, innocently enough, whether he did not feel that 'sterile academic eclecticism' dogged his path, Johnson replied that the danger was the opposite; the sterility of the 'Academy of the Modern Movement'. He went on to claim that the only absolute of the present was change, 'There are no rules, surely no certainties in any of the arts. There is only the feeling of a wonderful freedom'.[16]

The fourth crutch was that of COMFORT, a simple term which Johnson equated with environmental control in its most scientific form, a concept which—in turn—he traced back to John Stuart Mill and utilitarianism. In a telling example he explained the loss of *sensible* comfort that the creation of objective environmental comfort could entail.

> 'The fireplace, for example, is out of place in the controlled environment of the house. It heats up and throws off thermostats. But I like the beauty of a fireplace so I keep my thermostat way down to sixty, and then I light a big roaring fire so I can move back and forth. Now that's not a controlled environment. *I* control the environment. It's a lot more fun.'[17]

Such uncharacteristically crackerbarrel philosophizing was abandoned for the fifth crutch, CHEAPNESS. Here, in the Bourbon vein for which he later became notorious, he decried economic achievements as aspects of architecture. 'Realism' as applied to the high-intensity use of space in both commercial and private development seemed to him to be an achievement indeed, but primarily in economic terms—not architectural. To represent the construction of a 25,000-dollar house as an architectural triumph was to misunderstand the very purpose and meaning of architecture. The same was true of the sixth crutch—SERVING THE CLIENT. Here he confronted the notion that human values could be interpreted through client's requirements by claiming that such expediency was at best an excuse for the relinquishing of responsibility to the art of architecture. The seventh and last crutch, reliance upon the dictates of STRUCTURE, seemed to him to summarize the critical nature of the relationship between architects and twentieth-century technology —a relationship which he correctly identified as central to any dispute about the role of architecture at the present time. Here he attempted to deal with the heresy raised by Buckminster Fuller, at that time—as now —an influential figure amongst students. Fuller had since the late 1920s been proselytizing for a concept of space-enclosing technology derived equally from ecologically and scientifically determined world needs. According to Fuller—to whom the award of the Gold Medal of the Royal Institute of British Architects (RIBA) for 1968 Johnson was to deplore on the ground that Fuller 'loathes architecture in the heart of his being'[18]—buildings should be constructed according to the same principles of lightness and strength as govern the design of boats or aircraft. 'How much does your house *weigh*?' was Fuller's favourite question, to which an audience of architectural students could give no answer, or if they could were condemned to endure a lengthy denunciation of the waste of raw materials exemplified by the most menial product of 'architecture'. The strength of Fuller's case, which in the years since the publication of 'The Seven Crutches of Modern Architecture' in 1955 has grown considerably, was even then undeniable. Johnson's refutation of it depended upon a semantic and cultural argument. First he noted that the products of an engineer's analysis of environmental needs should not be termed architecture. Architecture as he saw it had an impeccable pedigree extending back to antiquity, it was a cultural matter, as remote from considerations of weight and cost as is the message of the Bible from the quality of the paper it is printed on, or from the quality of its binding. To ask how much the Great Pyramid of Cheops *weighs*, and to demonstrate that ten thousand Pharaohs could have been buried at greater speed and at less cost using aluminium tubes, seemed to Johnson to represent the final dislocation of the meaning and value of culture. Creation, in the cultural context he saw, was a solitary and ennobling experience far removed from formulae of any kind, unless it be those hallowed traditions of knowledge surrounding the processional rituals upon which the concept of human dignity was founded. It was here that the engineering efficiency of the type of structure which Fuller proposed collided most directly with his own creative vision. Speaking of Buckminster Fuller, Johnson said that he

'talks, you know, for five or six hours, and he ends up that all architecture is nonsense, and you have to build something like discontinuous domes . . . Have you ever seen Bucky trying to put a door into one of his domed buildings? He's never succeeded, and wisely, when he does them, he doesn't put any covering on them, so they are magnificent pieces of pure sculpture. Sculpture alone cannot result in architecture because architecture has problems that Bucky Fuller has not faced, like how do you get in and out.'[19]

To this a Fuller protagonist might reply that only Johnson's cultured man, bearing centuries of tradition upon his back, would see difficulties in getting in and out of a dome. The eskimo, the North American Indian, the driver of a Mercedes Benz 300SL, the crew of a Lunar Excursion Module see no difficulty here. Two different concepts of human dignity, two different cultures are expressed in this exchange, and the polarity has intensified since 1955.

With the two years of collaboration over the enormous Seagram Building, Johnson entered a new phase of his career. He acquired a large office staff and a model-making workshop; like Mies he worked extensively with models, building the first suggestions himself in plastic or cardboard, then modifying or improving the concept on models built to a larger scale. Again like Mies he grew to enjoy the ritual of studying the model from different viewpoints, instructing an assistant to turn it this way and that whilst he sat impassive at his desk.[20] Johnson grew during the years following the completion of the Seagram restaurant in 1959 to employ his assistants solely as executives. Discussions, invitations of opinion, suggestions from employees, all were eschewed. The staff turnover in his office became and remains high. Assistants, many of them foreign, worked for him in order to say that they had worked for him; he employed them because his method is as ancient as the practice of architecture itself. He became a 'form giver' in the grand tradition. One former employee recalls incorporating some ideas of his own into a sketch Johnson gave him to work up. 'I am not interested in your ideas', was Johnson's response upon inspecting the work; the assistant was transferred to other tasks.[21] One is put in mind of the reply to Adolf Placzek's inquiry of a psychoanalyst as to why architects were known for longevity: 'Of course they live long—because they have a chance to act out their aggressions'.[22]

In the decade following the completion of the Seagram Building Johnson's enlarged practice and lionized status in New York society enabled him to develop both an oracular style of speech and argument, and an increasingly monumental body of work. He abandoned both his earlier timidity and the 'eighth crutch'—the Miesian vernacular within which he had worked until that time.[23] Alterations and additions at New Canaan followed, the chief of which was the construction of a small pavilion and fountain on the lake below the guest house. A high stone wall concealing the house from the road altogether conspired with a new arrangement of approach paths to invest the use of the house with more formalized patterns of movement than ever. The approach to the pavilion—a building itself deliberately undersized in order to exaggerate its distance from the house—was carefully arranged so as to provide glimpses of both fountain and structure from an angular path occasionally turning back on itself and finally crossing the stream at the head of the lake by means of a footbridge. However, these operations were but small-scale models of what Johnson hoped to achieve in the public realm; in the early 1960s he and his partner Richard Foster were commissioned to design the New York State Theater, itself part of the Lincoln Center which has been heavily criticized in recent years. The commission was split up according to the function of the buildings in the complex, Harrison and Abramovitz being awarded the Metropolitan Opera House and Philharmonic Hall respectively, whilst other architects received ancillary buildings. From the first Johnson attempted to co-ordinate all the designs around a massive public space; he proposed a great square defined on three sides by a tall colonnade of piers with open networked capitals. His own theatre and Abramovitz's hall would have their principal façades formed by this colonnade whilst the opera house at the rear would have provided the dominant central feature. This grand plan was not accepted although in the event both Johnson's theatre and Abramovitz's hall were built with tall porticos. The opera house at the rear was not related with them and the square itself had no entrance to the front such as the colonnade would have provided. Processional grasp, as evidenced at New Canaan and in later additions to the Museum of Modern Art, was confined to the interior of Johnson's theatre. It may have been that the difficulties he experienced here, allied to similar complexities which were later to afflict another large project for Washington Square, led Johnson more clearly to enunciate his conception of the importance of monumentality in the architectural expressions of modern America. For Johnson the concept of a processional whole, of which buildings were a part and within which people progressed according to defined paths, was a profound truth which the multiplicity of interests in the American urban scene served only to frustrate and confuse. 'Architecture', he observed in 1965, 'is surely not the design of space, certainly not the massing or organisation of volumes. These are ancillary to the main point which is the organisation of procession. Architecture exists only in *time*.' The time taken for movement within and without buildings was of course in the most literal sense a function of size; no matter what ingenuities of route and scale were built into the New Canaan house they could never transcend the *smallness* of the whole and the consequent brevity of the architectural experience to which they amounted in sum. His whole conception of architecture (after his Miesian apprenticeship was at an end) required size and scale in order to express a truly symphonic variety of expression, and here modern American seemed always to frustrate him. Only in the cloistered society of the university was he able to seize control and patronage of a grand enough order to develop his plans, but here—as in the myriad private houses he had built—the smallness of scale seemed to mock his efforts. Longing to be able to work on a scale which could be compared to that of the architects of ancient Greece and Rome or of the Renaissance, Johnson was compelled to exercize his talents in the almost monastic seclusion of the private or the semi-private realm. At Yale, where the Pierson-Sage science area offered a comprehensive challenge, he was able to erect three closely related buildings, but even here the constraints imposed by the existing adjacent buildings were formidable. On the one hand stood the nineteenth-century houses of Hillhouse Avenue and on the other a number of science buildings erected over the years, including a large block of industrial appearance and a mainly subterranean nuclear research centre. Originally intending five buildings, Johnson in the end concentrated on a tower of seventeen storeys to achieve his principal effect. The tower was sited at the corner of a walled terrace of rectangular shape and its aspect was carefully considered from the point of view of approach. Hitchcock quotes Johnson as follows.

'What I intend is space seen in motion. A walk with change in direction with changing objectives. Also a slipping by of the people like a Giacometti "Place" . . . You cannot, I hope, for a second be confused, or worse, annoyed in the turnings. You are forced to the entry of the tower.'[24]

And so you are forced also into an appreciation of the architecture and a sensible rather than intellectual comprehension of its purpose.

By a curious irony of fate the America into which Johnson grew in his maturity expressed within its culture both the acceptance and the rejection of his vision. One part of the nation's consciousness rejects utterly the kind of physical determinism which Johnson sees as the great achievement of historic architecture; an arrangement of buildings which subliminally compels certain directions and courses of action compels also attitudes of respect and wonder, perhaps even love. There is growing in America today both a repudiation of such reinforcement of power by form, and an increasing reliance upon it by those institutions and individuals who in the past received respect as a matter of course and now find themselves obliged to insist upon it as a duty. In bewailing the absence of monumentality in American building and in pointing out that the founding fathers of that nation built their public buildings at proportionally greater cost and effort than do their present-day successors, Johnson adumbrated courses of action which are all too clearly being followed in the baroque public life of the world's most affluent nation. The Lyndon Baines Johnson Memorial Library in Dallas, Texas, designed by Gordon Bunshaft, and the Kennedy Center for the Performing Arts in Washington, D.C., designed by Edward Stone, may well represent merely the beginning of a Pharaonic tendency amongst the powerful in America. If it does then it is establishing a thesis against which an antithesis is already evident. In that very failure to seize control of immense urban projects in the manner of his illustrious predecessors, Johnson is demonstrating not so much his own failure as the difference between the modern and the ancient world. His architecture is circumscribed—in time as well as space.

1 'Talking to Philip Johnson', *Building Design*, 10 August 1970

2 Usually attributed to the Johnson-Hitchcock partnership, the term 'International Style' is ascribed by Peter Blake (in *The Master Builders*, London, 1960) to 'the Museum of Modern Art's leading spirit, Alfred Barr'.

3 See Martin Pawley, *Mies van der Rohe*, London and New York 1970

4 Henry-Russell Hitchcock, *Philip Johnson, Architecture 1949–65*, London and New York, 1966; John M. Jacobus, Jr, *Philip Johnson*, New York and London, 1962

5 *Building Design*, 10 August 1970

6 See letter to Jürgen Joedicke in Jacobus, op. cit. (see note 4)

7 Philip Johnson, *Mies van der Rohe*, Museum of Modern Art, New York, 1947; second edition with additional material, 1953

8 Henry-Russell Hitchcock, 'The Current Work of Philip Johnson', *Zodiac* VIII, 1961, p. 66

9 'House at New Canaan, Connecticut, architect Philip Johnson', *The Architectural Review* CVIII, No. 645, September 1950, pp. 152–60; this contains the architect's own comments on his sources of inspiration

10 'The Seven Crutches of Modern Architecture', *Perspecta* III, 1955

11 Philippe Boudon, *Pessac de Le Corbusier*, Paris, 1969

12 'The Seven Crutches of Modern Architecture', *Perspecta* III, 1955

13 The Japanese writer Naibu Akashi in his book *Philip Johnson*, Tokyo, 1968, reports having crab pilaff ordered for him by Johnson in the Four Seasons Restaurant; Akashi was not even shown the menu

14 *Building Design*, 10 August 1970

15 Ibid.

16 Letter to Jürgen Joedicke in Jacobus, op. cit. (see note 4)

17 'The Seven Crutches of Modern Architecture', *Perspecta* III, 1955

18 *Building Design*, 10 August 1970

19 'The Seven Crutches of Modern Architecture', *Perspecta* III, 1955

20 Peter Blake, *The Master Builders*, London, 1960

21 Naibu Akashi, op. cit.

22 Quoted in Henry-Russell Hitchcock, op. cit.

23 Ibid.

24 Ibid.

The Plates

1-9, The Glass House, New Canaan, Conn. (1949)

1 The main façade at the end of the approach walk; cars are parked some distance away

2 Plan of the house showing brick fireplace/ablution tower and approach path

3 View showing the combined reflectivity and transparency of the glass walls, black-painted steel frame and brick plinth

4 Interior showing wood-block flooring, brick tower to right, and chairs designed by Mies van der Rohe

1

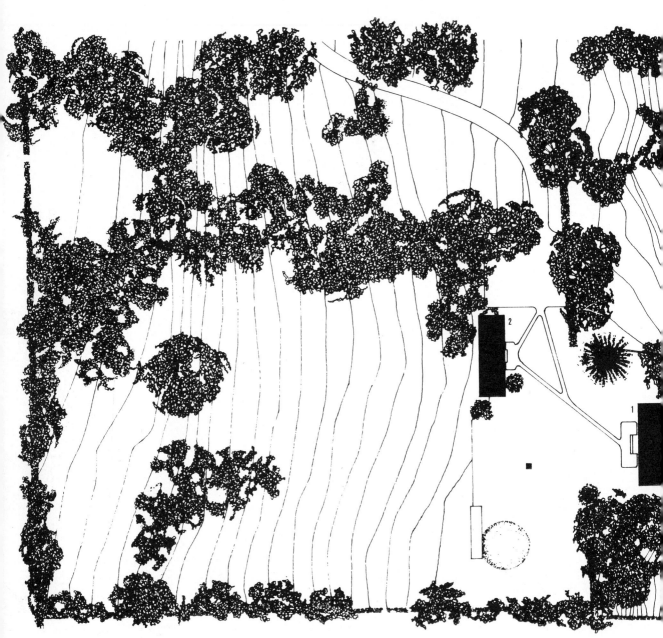

5 The entire New Canaan site
showing: 1, Glass House; 2,
guest house, added in solid brick
to counterpoint the transparency
of the main house; 3, the 6ft-high
pavilion (added in 1962) set on the
small lake and reached by a foot-
path. Later additions (not shown)
were an underground art gallery
(1965) and a glass-covered
sculpture gallery (1970)

6 View towards guest hou
from Glass House

7 Interior of the guest-house
bedroom with wall drapes and
canopied falsework

8 The pavilion seen from the belt of trees beneath the guest house; the small scale of the pavilion (6ft high) creates an illusion in respect of the size of the lake

9 Plan of pavilion showing diminutive size

8

9

0   2m

10-13, Richard Hodgson house, New Canaan, Conn. (1951)

10 Plan of the Hodgson house showing partially enclosed court and corridor linking house and guest house

11 View from the north showing courtyard, corridor to guest house (right), and projecting living-room chimney on the left

12 The corridor linking main house and guest house

13 The partially enclosed court with glazed walls

10

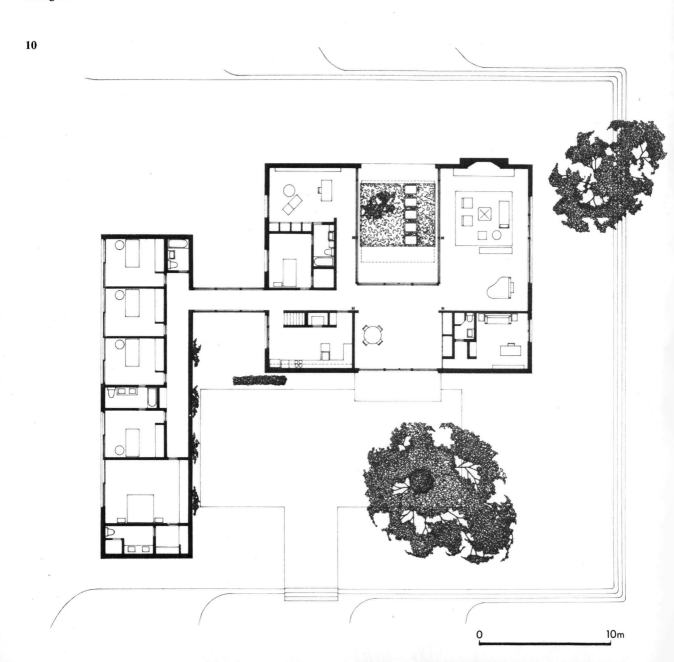

0   10m

14-16, Eric Boissonnas house, New Canaan, Conn. (1956)

14 View of the Boissonnas house from base of hilltop ridge; the double-height living room is partly obscured by trees to the left

15 Plan of the house showing square grid and brick piers

16 The single-storey entrance level with living area to the rear overlooking slope

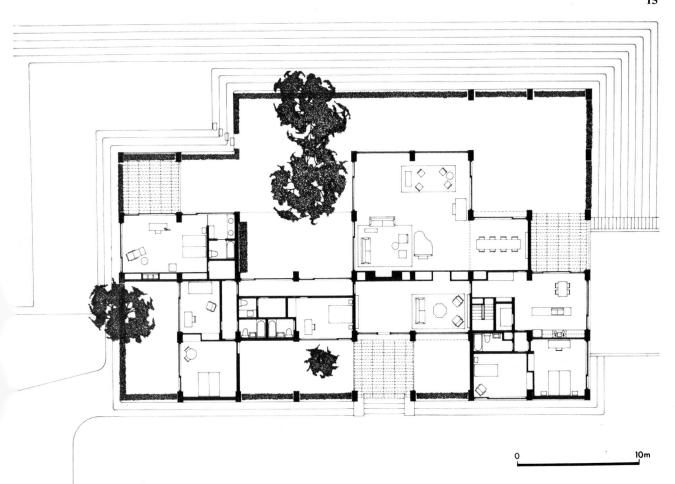

0   10m

17-22, Kneses Tifereth Israel Synagogue, Port Chester, N.Y. (1956)

17 View of the main façade of the synagogue

18 Section through elliptical entrance porch and rectangular main hall

19 Plan of the synagogue showing auxiliary accommodation in low block to the rear

20 Interior of the auditorium; the false ceiling is noteworthy

21 Detail of vaulted falsework

22 Interior showing coloured glass set in wall slits and apparent vaulting

17

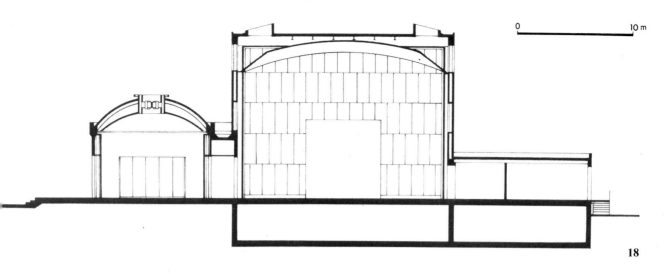

18

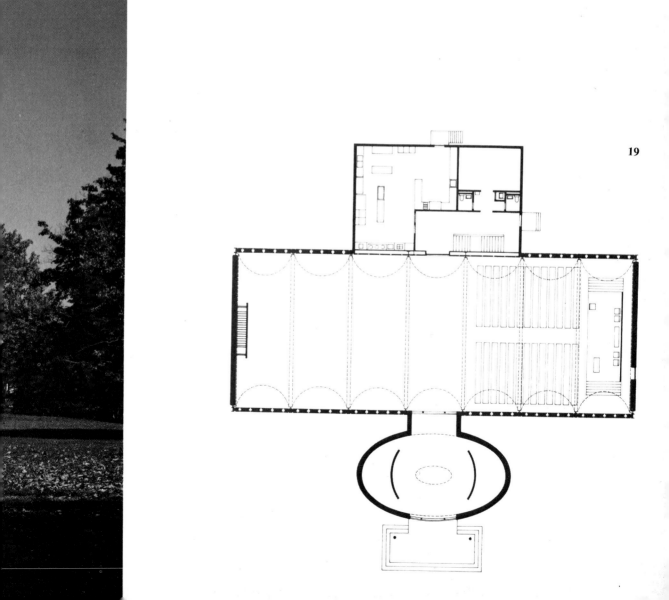

19

**23-26, University of St Thomas,
Houston, Texas (1957)**

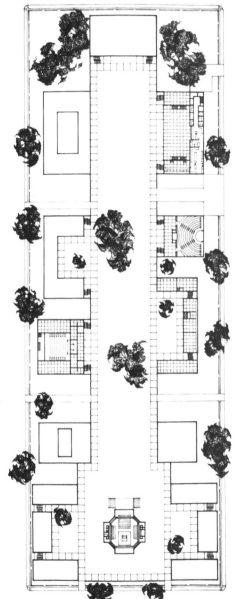

23 Plan of university campus
showing buildings on either side of
the central open spine

24 Double-level circulation galleries

25 The outline framing and brick
infill which is carried through the
entire arrangement of buildings

26 Detail of façade

23

24

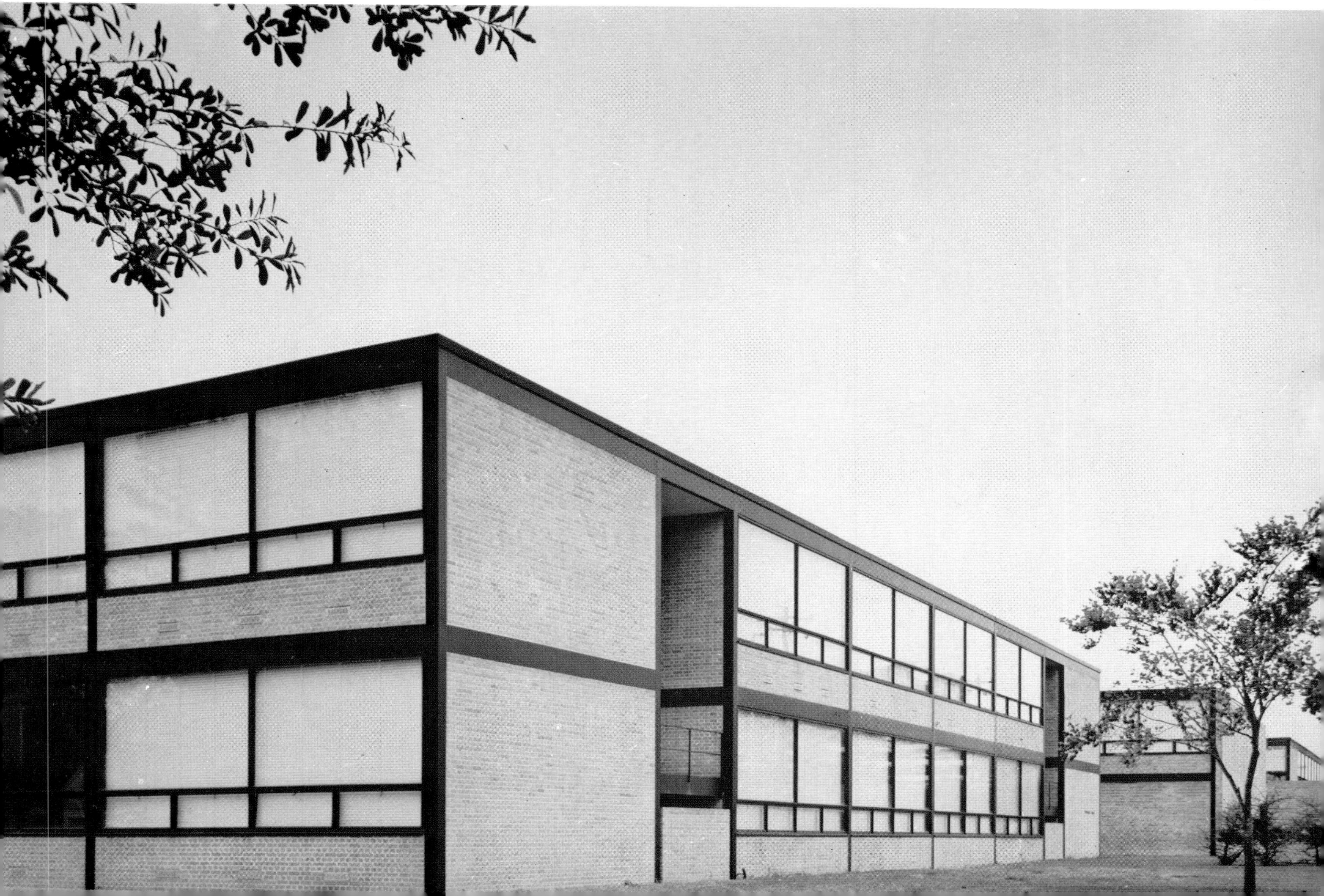

27, 28, Asia House, New York, N.Y. (1959)

27 The glazed façade contrasting
with nineteenth-century neighbours

28 Detail showing revolving door
entrance

**29-31, Four Seasons Restaurant,
Seagram Building,
New York, N.Y. (1959)**

29 'Curtains' made from chains of
anodised aluminium

30 Part of the interior showing
pool, and chairs designed by Mies
van der Rohe

31 Interior view showing
suspended sculpture by Lippold
and lavish appointments

29

32-40, Munson-Williams-Proctor Institute, Utica, N.Y. (1960)

32 The main entrance bridging a dry moat. Massive granite facings and bronze-sheathed piers can be clearly seen

33 The central hall showing suspended gallery

34 The staircase leading to the gallery

35 Central hall and entrance seen from the gallery

36

36 Detail of steel balustrading in
fine vertical elements

37 Coffered roof-lights above the
central hall

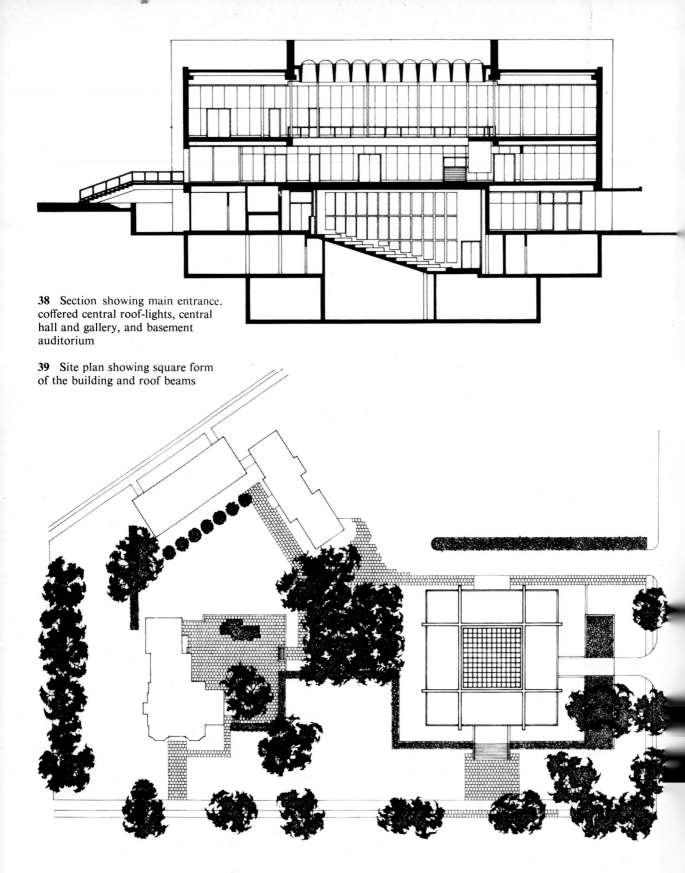

38 Section showing main entrance, coffered central roof-lights, central hall and gallery, and basement auditorium

39 Site plan showing square form of the building and roof beams

40 Interior of an artificially lit gallery on the perimeter of the building

41

41-45, Amon Carter Museum of Western Art, Fort Worth, Texas (1961)

41 The façade seen from the highway

42 Site plan showing public approach via processional path

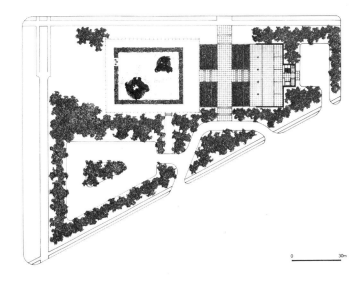

0   30m

43

43 Main entrance to the museum

44 Detail of shellstone portico

45 Interior of portico showing
opaque glazing, recessed lighting,
and overall cloister-like effect

**46-54, Sheldon Memorial
Art Gallery, Lincoln, Nebraska
(1963)**

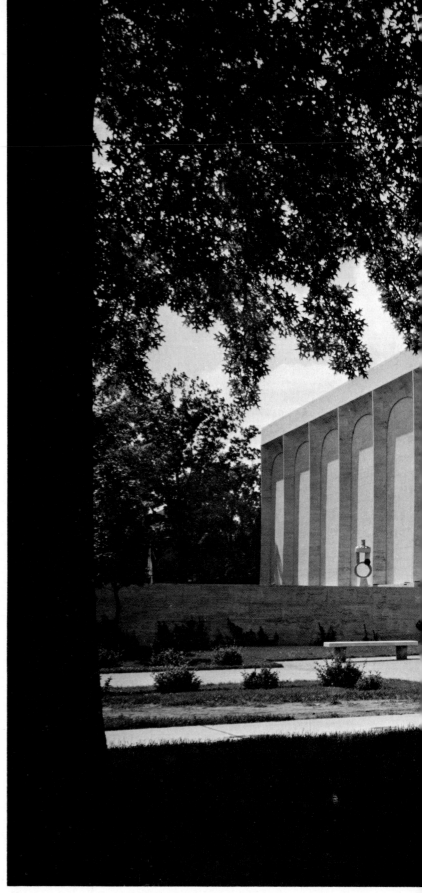

46 The two-storey travertine
columns which become pilasters
on either side of the entrance

47 The entrance portico showing well-studied sciagraphy and fluted columns

48 Section showing internal two-storey hall and central staircase

49, 50 Ground- and first-floor plans

51 Staircase up from entrance hall, with columns of portico beyond glazed entrance

52 First-floor gallery spanning the central hall, with symmetrical access stair and view through rear portico

53 Stair access showing travertine interior finish and rib intersection on ceiling

54 Rectangular punctures in travertine wall and recessed lighting set into domed ceiling

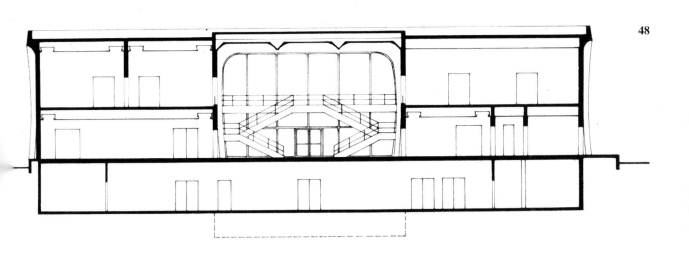

48

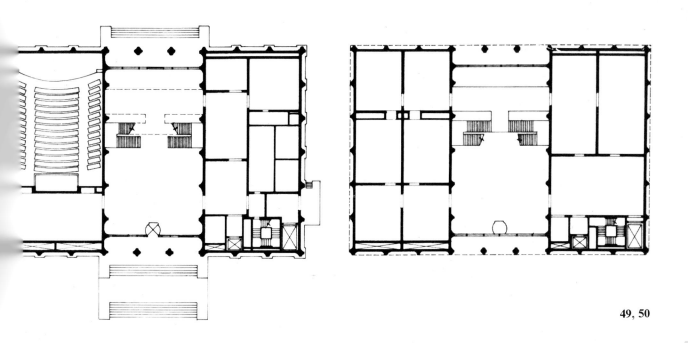

49, 50

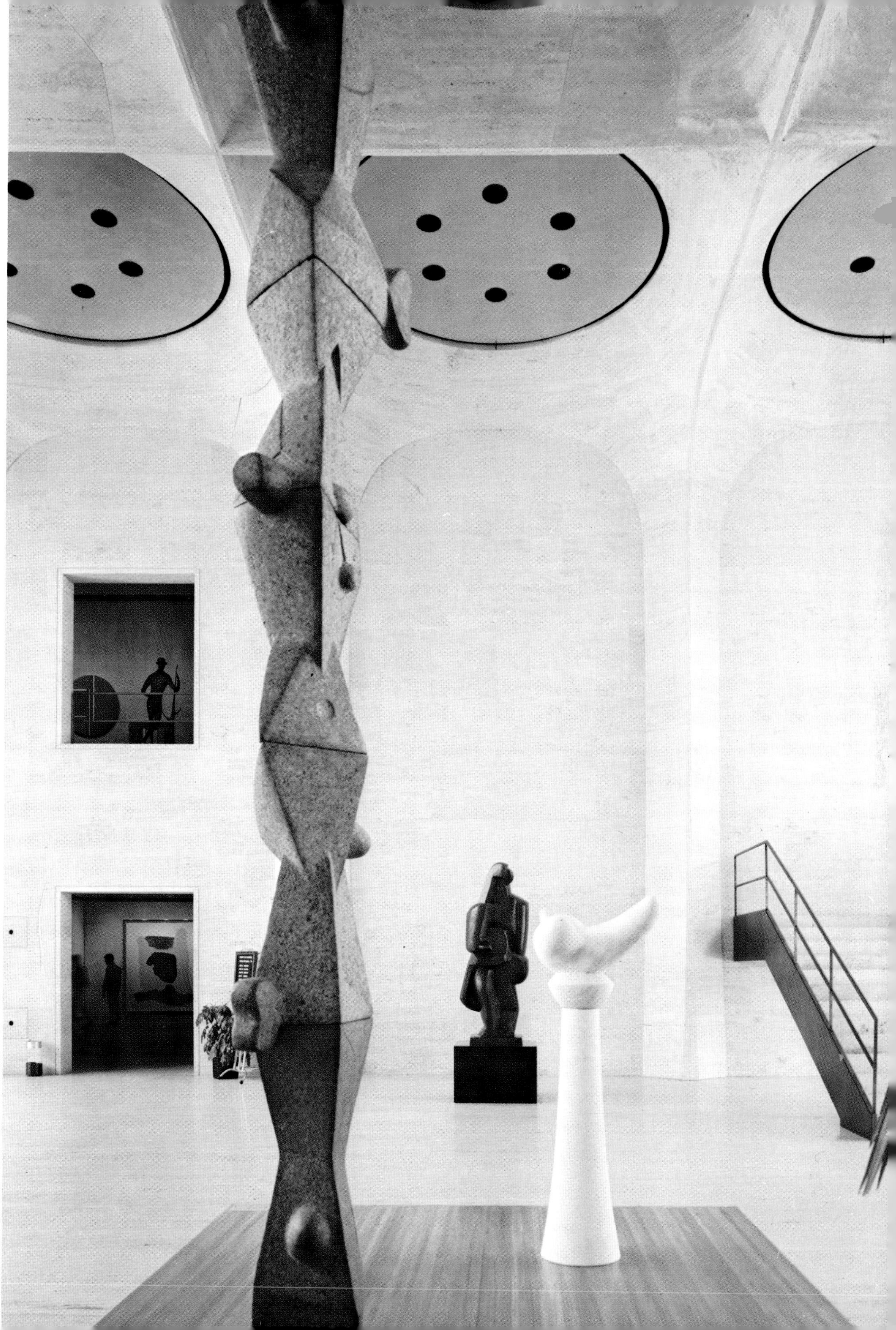

55 Site plan of the Museum of Modern Art, showing main building to left, annexe to right, and enlarged sculpture garden above

56 Façade of original building and annexe on 53rd Street, showing tinted glazing and contrasting horizontal and vertical emphasis

55

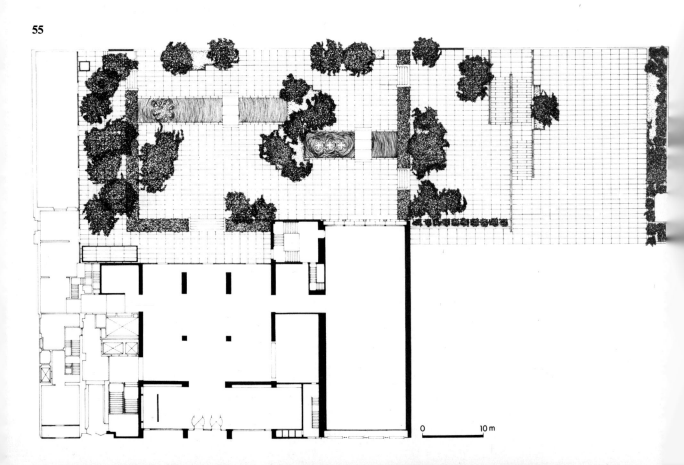

0   10 m

57

57 View of the annexe façade
from below

58 The sculpture garden

**59-64, New York State Theater,
Lincoln Center, New York, N.Y.
(1964)**

59 The forecourt and main
entrance to the theatre, with
computercontrolled fountain

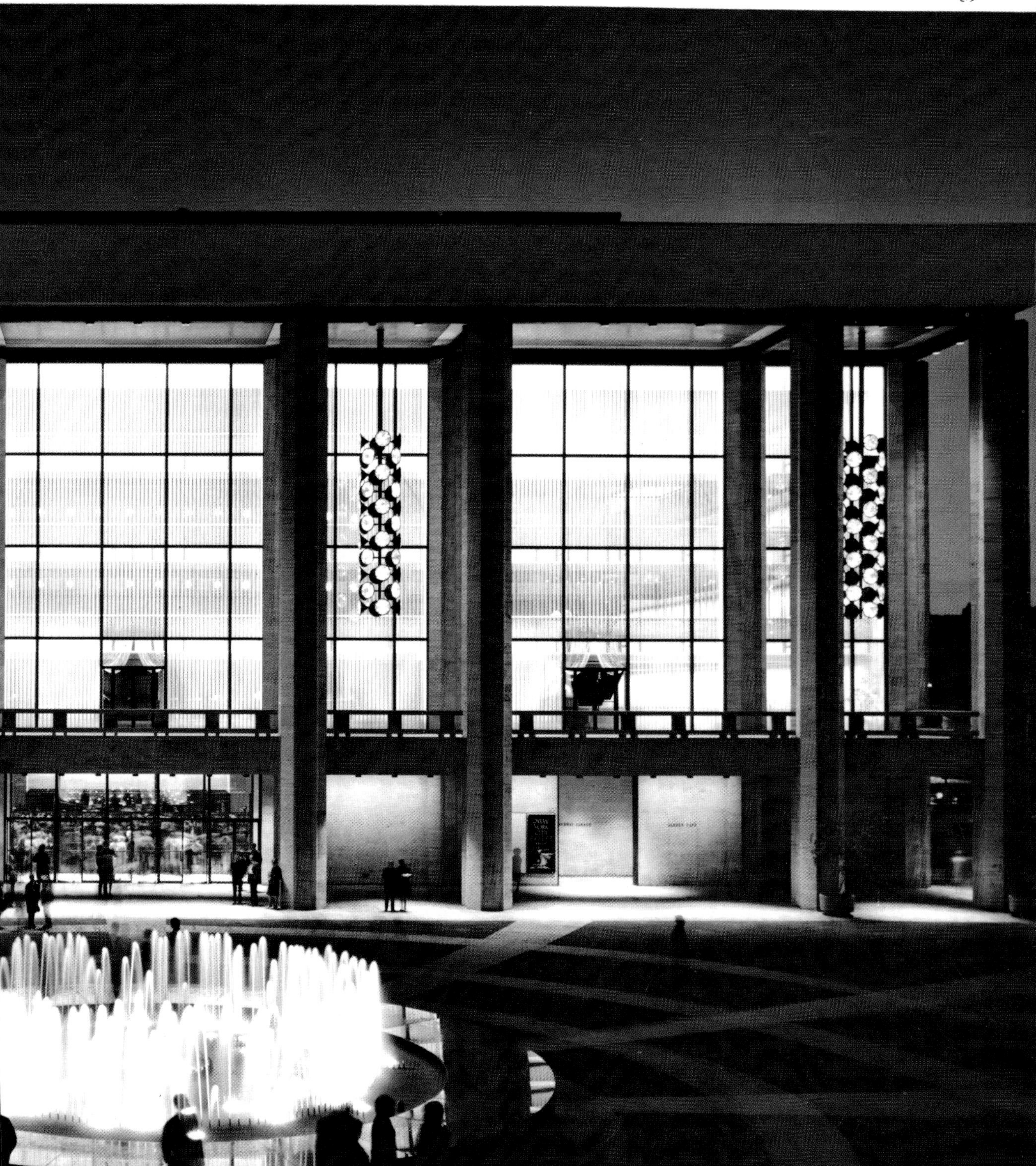

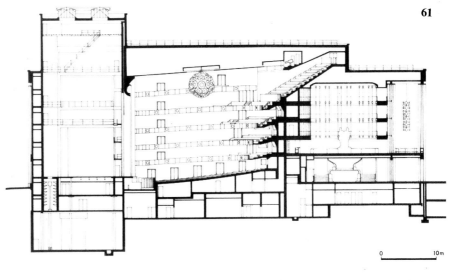

0   10m

60 The entrance hall showing curve of rear of auditorium at right, gold-leaf ceiling and sculptures

61 Section through auditorium and entrance hall at right

62 Interior of auditorium showing caged lighting ball

63, 64 Plans at balcony level and stalls at entrance level

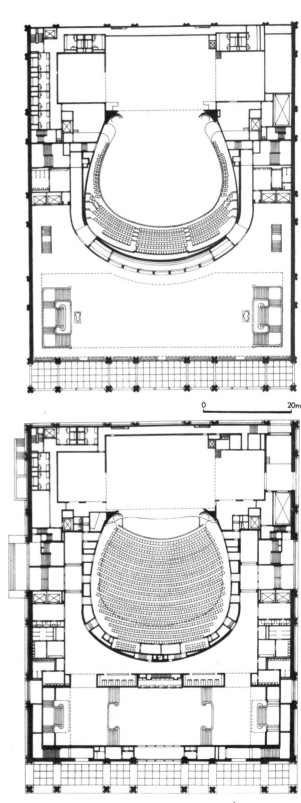

0   20m

63, 64

65-70, New York State Pavilion, World's Fair, Flushing, N.Y. (1964)

65

66

68   Detail of fins to perimeter ring
beam

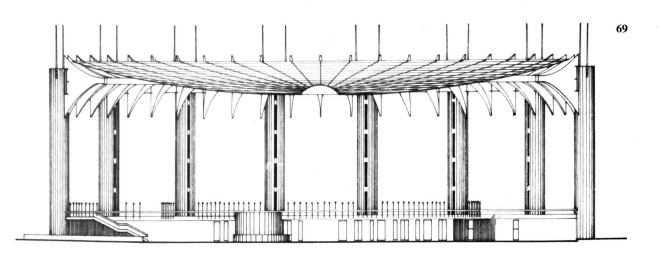

69

69   Section through pavilion

70   Plan of pavilion showing
outline map of New York State set
n floor-tiles

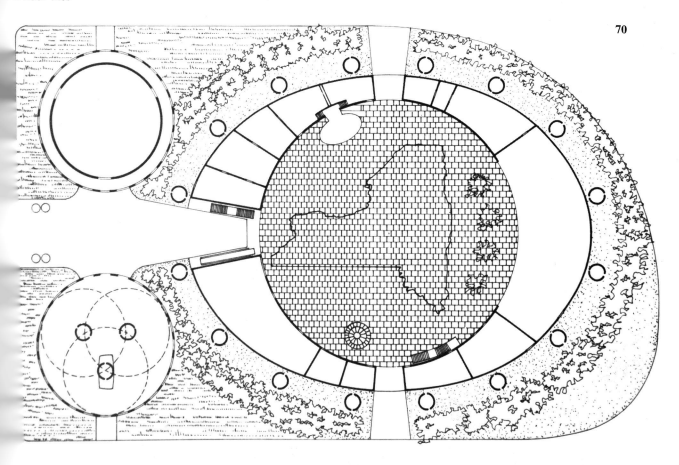

70

**71, 72, Epidemiology and Public Health Building,
Yale University, New Haven, Conn. (1965)**

71 Site plan showing duct columns
and recessed lower storey

72 An external view showing
external columns and obscured
lower floor

71

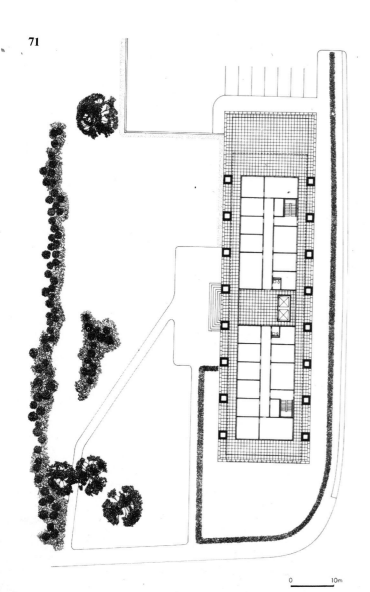

0   10m

72

73-76, Henry L. Moses Institute, Montefiore Hospital, New York N.Y. (1965)

73 Site plan showing massive columns incorporating ducting

74 Oblique view showing two symmetrical façades

75 Brick steps at the entrance to the glazed lower floor

76 The perimeter wall with tower overshooting

73

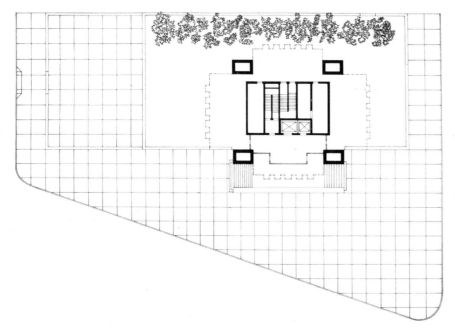

**77-85, Kline Science Center, Yale University,
New Haven, Conn. (1965)**

77 General view of the tower
from beyond the courtyard

78 Site plan showing court,
cloister and tower at top left

78

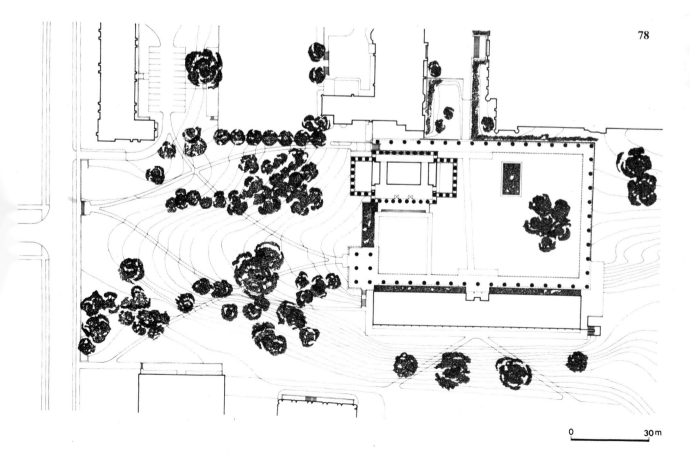

0   30 m

79 Façade showing brick-clad
vertical tubes

80 Detail of façade and entrance

81 The entrance hall, with external
columns

82 Library

83 Small courtyard with chair by
Breuer

84 Matching façade of adjacent
Geological Laboratories

85 Entrance staircase of the
Kline Science Center

Notes on the plates

1–9

The Glass House,
New Canaan, Conn. (1949)

Built as the architect's interpretation of Mies van der Rohe's concept of a glass-and-steel house—which itself first appeared as early as 1937 in the form of photomontages for an unrealized project for a house set mountainous country in Wyoming—Johnson's Glass House represents a cosmopolitanized adaptation of the original. It is sited within commuting distance of New York and has been steadily added to since its completion in 1949, two years ahead of Mies' own interpretation (the Farnsworth house, Plano, Ill.). Set on a closely cropped lawn, the house is a steel-frame structure with symmetrically opposed doors in all four walls. The steel frame is painted black, and the whole is raised on a plinth set amid trees with extensive views beyond. The glass walls respond to differing light conditions with varying degrees of reflectivity and transparency. A circular brick core encloses both fireplace and chimney and shower and lavatory. The remainder of the interior living space is open-planned.

10–13

Richard Hodgson house,
New Canaan, Conn. (1951)

This rectangular brick-and-glass composition features a courtyard enclosed on three sides with glazed walls giving on to it. The house/guest house combination is here directly linked by a glazed corridor but the overall effect is much less impressive than in the architect's own house. The house is reminiscent at once of projects by Mies van der Rohe and completed small houses by Marcel Breuer. The complex brick bonding and use of darker brick headers to create a patterned texture is noteworthy.

14–16

Eric Boissonnas house,
New Canaan, Conn. (1956)

This house is designed on a square grid plan marked out by substantial brick piers; it is larger than either of the two earlier houses illustrated, and features a double-height living room and a large external pergola. The house stands on a flattened hilltop and commands fine views over wooded country. The progression from external to internal spaces in the Boissonnas house represents a development from the Glass House that is, in the view of most critics, retrograde, with echoes of villas built in Potsdam in the nineteenth century by the German architect Karl Friedrich Schinkel. As in all earlier houses the method of construction is simple as well as evident.

17–22

Kneses Tifereth Israel
Synagogue, Port Chester, N.Y.
(1956)

Likened inaptly by some critics to the work of the French architect Claude Nicolas Ledoux, this building does yet retain something of an aura of late eighteenth-century academic projects about its massing and section. The isolated clarity, but not the form of the elliptical entrance porch linked to the rectangular body of the main building, may invite comparisons with late classical buildings, but the slit penetration of the concrete-block walls of the main building, combined with the expressed concrete columns give the whole an excessive and modern lightness—an effect which is even more emphasized by the interior. The curved false ceiling and spare, Klee-like reredos evoke irreverent memories of the bedroom in the guest house at New Canaan (pl. 7). The massive quality of the domed entrance porch is likewise weakened by the light canopy breaking the large entrance opening and by the lamp clusters on either side of the doors.

23–26
University of St Thomas,
Houston, Texas (1957)

A somewhat vernacular work, closely resembling contemporary college and school structures by Paul Rudolph and others, the University of St Thomas is built along a single open spine with covered ways on either side. The configuration allows for the intended linear expansion of the university to accommodate a maximum of 1,500 students, the present number being less than 500. The entire campus is constructed on a square module using brick walls and steel columns. Circulation is by open galleries at two levels, the effect created being that of an unglazed façade by Mies van der Rohe.

27, 28
Asia House, New York, N.Y.
(1959)

Designed concurrently with the Four Seasons Restaurant in the Seagram Building, this all-glazed façade in a predominantly residential district represents a version chosen from the three schemes which Johnson prepared. The first of these was a sculptural façade rejected by the client; the second, a bronze frame derived from the Seagram Building, was found to be too expensive; and the third was a steel frame with glazing bars picked out in white. The building represents Johnson's design at its most slavishly Miesian.

29–31
Four Seasons Restaurant,
Seagram Building,
New York, N.Y. (1959)

This interior design, executed at a cost of 4,500,000 dollars, is located on the first floor of the Seagram Building. Echoing Mies' external bronze cladding, the interior columns are faced in bronze whilst the walls are surfaced in a thick French walnut veneer. Tapestries by Miró and Picasso compete with 'curtains' formed from hundreds of thin chains of anodised aluminium and a considerable amount of shrubbery. A large rectangular pool is lined with marble.

   This lavish environment is generally regarded as Johnson's last commission to be carried out according to design principles deriving directly from Mies van der Rohe.

32–40
Munson-Williams-Proctor
Institute, Utica, N.Y. (1960)

Far more successfully than the Kneses Tifereth Synagogue, this museum building captures a massive, ancient monumentality utterly alien to Mies van der Rohe's Crown Hall at the Illinois Institute of Technology (1952) or the Cullinan Museum of Fine Arts (1958). This is the emergence of Johnson's own dynastic style incorporating thematic elements from ancient Egypt as well as from the twentieth century. The granite-faced museum is suspended from four pairs of equidistant bronze-sheathed piers which are cranked as upstands to support the roof. The interior gallery ringing the central hall is suspended from these roof beams by tensile members.

41–45
Amon Carter Museum
of Western Art,
Fort Worth, Texas (1961)

This small museum was built for a millionaire with a collection of Western (as in cowboy) art; the façades formed from five arches of hand-sculpted Texas shellstone. Dark tinted windows behind the arches create the impression of a void, and approach planning ensures that the one-directional portico forms the only public entrance.

46–54
Sheldon Memorial Art Gallery,
Lincoln, Nebraska (1963)

This travertine-columned museum is one of Johnson's grandiloquent buildings. It illustrates his employment of vitiated classical and neo-classical forms, merging column, capital and entablature into one smooth, curvilinear form, and thereby losing altogether the articulation perfected by the ancients over many centuries. The result here is an effete form of engineering arch such as might naturally emerge from the use of polystyrene instead of marble. Some attention (reminiscent of an earlier age) was devoted to this formal aspect, the arches being test-erected in Italy in order to assess the play of sunlight upon them. The flowing of normally discrete elements into one another is carried through the blank wall panels between the columns and the flat cornice itself, all of which are in travertine.

55–58
The Museum of Modern Art
Annexe, New York, N.Y.
(1964)

Johnson's extension to the original building (1939) on 53rd Street by Goodwin and Stone is a radical departure from the original Corbusian structure. It features a Miesian façade of dark-painted steel and tinted glass but with uncharacteristic rounded corners to the frames and a strong vertical emphasis. The sculpture garden to the rear of the main building has been modified extensively since its introduction in 1953. It marks a considerable extension of Johnson's processional theory, with several interconnected walks, and a wall against 54th Street of increased height.

59–64
New York State Theater,
Lincoln Center,
New York, N.Y. (1964)

The New York State Theater is the surviving part of an earlier scheme in which Johnson attempted to co-ordinate an Opera House and Philharmonic Hall as well; the theatre project represented Johnson's largest commission at that time. The entrance lies between paired columns and gives on to a high entrance hall featuring a gold-leaf ceiling. From the hall a staircase leads into the auditorium—the curve of whose rear wall has the effect of projecting into the high entrance hall. The auditorium itself is of traditional form with four balconies.

65–70
New York State Pavilion,
World's Fair,
Flushing, New York (1964)

This open circular structure has a multicoloured vinyl roof supported on tension wires between the perimeter ring beam and a central ring, the whole being supported by cylindrical concrete towers. Designed for the 1964 exposition, it has not been demolished since; as the plan shows, a map of the State of New York is incorporated in the floor tiling. To the right of the main entrance are three location towers of different heights.

71, 72
Epidemiology and Public Health
Building, Yale University,
New Haven, Conn. (1965)

Like the Utica museum (pls 32–40), this building is a massive block
seemingly suspended by huge columns, although in this case they are
greater in number and do not project vertically as roof beams. The uni-
form stone cladding of columns and walls creates an even more massive
impression, reinforced by the oversizing of the columns themselves,
which also house vertical ducts. The ground floor is glazed *in toto,* but
with tinted glass and dark paint so that it retreats visually into opacity.

73–76
Henry L. Moses Institute,
Montefiore Hospital,
New York, N.Y. (1965)

In this remarkable tower, which serves as a medical laboratory, servicing
and functional elements such as ducts and windows are allowed to
determine the massive form of the brick-clad structure. As in earlier
designs the recessed and obscured lower storey is present but here its
effect is quite different as a result of the *trompe l'œil* caused by the
conversion of the four main columns into a solid brick box above tenth-
storey level. The ribs on each façade are formed alternately from windows and ducts.

77–85
Kline Science Center,
Yale University,
New Haven, Conn. (1965)

One of Johnson's most famous processional achievements, the Kline
tower springing from its courtyard employs the same overall symmetry
as the Henry L. Moses Institute, but with vertical circular elements clad
in glazed brick and rising to seventeen storeys. These elements are ducts
as before; their form is continued as a cloister around the courtyard in
which the tower stands. The massing and proportions of the tower are
reminiscent of Adler and Sullivan's Guaranty building at Buffalo, N.Y.
(1895). The cylindrical elements are, however, too ruthlessly employed
without horizontal emphasis for the comparison to be more than super-
ficial.

Chronological list: projects and events

1906 Born 8 July at Cleveland, Ohio, son of Homer H. and Louise Pope Johnson

1923–30 Studies at Harvard University

1930–36 Director of the Department of Architecture at the Museum of Modern Art, New York

1932 Publication of *The International Style: architecture since 1922*

1942 Architect's own house, Cambridge, Mass.

1943 Qualifies as an architect at the Graduate School of Design, Harvard University

1946–54 Director of the Department of Architecture and Design at the Museum of Modern Art, New York

1946 Booth house, Bedford Village, N.Y.; Farney house, Sagaponack, Long Island, N.Y.

1947 His book *Mies van der Rohe* published by the Museum of Modern Art, New York

1949 Glass House, New Canaan, Conn.; Paine house, Willsboro, N.Y.; Wolf house, Newburgh, N.Y.

1950 Annexe to the Museum of Modern Art, New York; de Menil house, Houston, Texas; Rockefeller guest house, New York

1951 Hodgson house, New Canaan, Conn. (co-architect, Landes Gores); Oneto house, Livingston, N.Y.

1952 Schlumberger Administration Building, Ridgefield, Conn.

1953 Abby Aldrich Rockefeller sculpture garden, Museum of Modern Art, New York; Ball house and Wiley house, both New Canaan, Conn.

1954 Davis house, Wayzata, Minn.

1955 Hirshhorn house, Ontario, Canada; Meteor Crater pavilion, Arizona; Wiley Development Co. house, New Canaan, Conn.

1956 Boissonnas house, New Canaan, Conn.; Leonhardt house, Lloyd's Neck, Long Island, N.Y.; Kneses Tifereth Synagogue, Fort Chester, N.Y.

1957 University of St Thomas, Houston, Texas; Seton Hill College dormitory, Greensburg, Pa.

1959 Asia House, New York; Four Seasons Restaurant, Seagram Building, New York
1960 Munson-Williams-Proctor Institute, Utica, N.Y.; nuclear reactor, Rehovot, Israel; Roofless Church, New Harmony, Ind.; Tourre house, Vaucresson, France; Sarah Lawrence College dormitories, Bronxville, N.Y.
1961 Amon Carter Museum of Western Art, Fort Worth, Texas; Brown University Computing Center, Providence, R.I.
1962 Pavilion, New Canaan, Conn.
1963 Museum for Pre-Columbian Art, Dumbarton Oaks, Washington, D.C.; Sheldon Memorial Art Gallery, University of Nebraska, Lincoln, Neb.; St Anselm's Abbey monastery wing, Washington, D.C.
1964 Beck house, Dallas, Texas; Boissonnas house, Cap Bénat, France; Kline Geology Laboratory, Yale University, New Haven, Conn.; east wing and garden wing, Museum of Modern Art, New York; New York State Theater, Lincoln Center, New York (with Richard Foster); New York State Pavilion, World's Fair, Flushing, N.Y. (with Richard Foster)
1965 Epidemiology and Public Health Building, Yale University, New Haven, Conn. (co-architect, Office of Douglas Orr); underground art gallery, New Canaan, Conn.; Kline Chemistry Laboratory and Kline Science Center, Yale University, New Haven, Conn.; Henry L. Moses Institute, Montefiore Hospital, New York; art gallery, Bielefeld, W. Germany; Geier house, Cincinnati, Ohio
1966 Projects for: Hendrix College library, Conway, Ark. (in association with Wittenberg, Delony and Davidson); memorial, Staten Island, N.Y.
1967 Projects for: Public Library extension, Boston, Mass.; sewage treatment plant, New York
1968 Project for Galleria, Washington Square, New York
1969 Project for Lehmann Bros. Building, New York
1970 Philip Johnson sculpture gallery, New Canaan, Conn.; project for Twin Towers, New York

Select bibliography

On Philip Johnson .

Blake, Peter, *The Master Builders*, London, 1960
Hitchcock, Henry-Russell, *Philip Johnson, Architecture 1949–65*, London and New York, 1966
Jacobus, John M., Jr, *Philip Johnson*, New York and London, 1962; *Twentieth Century Architecture 1940–65*, New York and London, 1966
Joedicke, Jürgen, *Architecture since 1945*, London, 1969
McCallum, Ian, *Architecture USA*, New York, 1959, and London, 1969
Stern, Robert, *New Directions in American Architecture,* London, 1969
Scully, Vincent, *American Architecture and Urbanism*, New York and London, 1969
Architectural Review, issues for September 1950 and April 1955

By Philip Johnson

The International Style: architecture since 1922 (with Henry-Russell Hitchcock), New York, 1932
Mies van der Rohe, Museum of Modern Art, New York, 1947; second edition, 1953
'The responsibility of the architect', *Perspecta* II, 1954
'The Seven Crutches of Modern Architecture', *Perspecta* III, 1955
'International Style—death or metamorphosis?', in Jacobus, John M., Jr, *Philip Johnson*, New York and London, 1962
'Whence and Whither: the processional element in architecture', *Perspecta* IX/X, 1965
'We shall not be thanked by posterity', *Fortune*, July 1966
'Talking to Philip Johnson', *Building Design*, 10 August 1970

Index